MAZECRAFT
ADVENTURE

Simon Ward

BARRON'S

Charlie Chimp

Ace McDanger

Astro Mouse

Jungle Jen

Indiana Bones

Hayley Comet

Doc Paradox

Robot ME2

First edition published in 2018
by Barron's Educational Series, Inc.

Copyright © 2017 by Arcturus Holdings Limited

First published in Great Britain in 2017 by Arcturus Publishing Limited
26/27 Bickels Yard, 151-153 Bermondsey Street
London SE1 3HA

All inquiries should be addressed to:
Barron's Educational Series, Inc.
250 Wireless Boulevard
Hauppauge, New York 11788
www.barronseduc.com

ISBN: 978-1-4380-1128-8

Editorial managers: Joe Harris and Becca Clunes
Project editor: Lisa Regan
Designer: Paul Oakley
Illustrators: Irina Golina-Sagatelian and Virginia Fontabona
Maze design: Simon Ward

Date of Manufacture: November 2017
Manufactured by: 1010 Printing, Hui Zhou City, China

Printed in China

9 8 7 6 5 4 3 2 1

Anna Kadabra

Kazam

Pongo

Captain Pegg

Avoid being caught by deadly creatures or fiendish traps!

Collect an item you'll need to reach your goal.

SHIPWRECK!

The ship's run aground! Sneak past the pirates and giant crabs to reach the island and rescue the treasure. Find the bucket of fish to fend off the sharks.

Collect all four treasure maps along the way and check them off.

Find the bucket of fish to feed the sharks.

START

32

33

Begin your adventure at the red START arrow.

Gather treasure, supplies, and precious items along the way.

Make your way to the yellow FINISH arrow.

MAGIC SCHOOL

Oh no, you are late for conjuring class and the classroom is locked! Find the magic key to open the locked door, but don't touch the gargoyle guardians.

FINISH

4

EVIL CLONES

Alert! Alert! The cloning machine is faulty. Dodge the evil clones to reach the "off" switch and stop the mayhem.

Collect all four bottles along the way and check them off.

START

FINISH

6

GORILLA GANG

Two of these gorillas are identical.
Can you spot them in this hairy gang?

SEA BATTLE

All hands on deck! Dodge the cannon fire and enemy pirates as you swashbuckle your way to the treasure. Watch out for the sharks!

FINISH

RODEO RANCH

Yeeha! There's a stampede in the corral. Can you pick up the coins and make it to the gate?

GRIDLOCK

Every row, column, and mini-grid should contain only one of each picture. Can you work out which ones fit in the empty squares?

JUNGLE RUN

Beware! Tigers and snakes! Criss-cross the piranha-infested river by canoe to get home safely to the treehouse.

Collect all four pineapples along the way and check them off.

ZOOM BROOM!

Hold on tight! Grab the floating scrolls while you race through the clouds, steering clear of the tornadoes to reach the rainbow.

Collect all four scrolls along the way and check them off.

FRAME GAME

Can you find a face for Ace?
Complete the picture by correctly
replacing the missing pieces in the frame.

ROCKET LAUNCH

The countdown has begun but the dopey droids are blocking the way. Switch the lever to unlock the red space gate so you can reach the rocket before blast off.

START

WHIRLPOOL

Here's a boat ride that will make you dizzy! Collect the treasure maps and escape the whirlpool without being eaten by sharks!

Collect all four treasure maps along the way and check them off.

HOCUS POCUS

These two tricksy wizards are almost identical, but not quite. Can you spot six differences between them?

LIONS' DEN

Grab four pineapples from the forest before the scary lions hunt you down!

Collect all four pineapples along the way and check them off.

START

FINISH

22

BOLT BURGER

Doc Paradox has made a nuts-and-bolts burger for his hungry robot! Use your crayons to complete the picture.

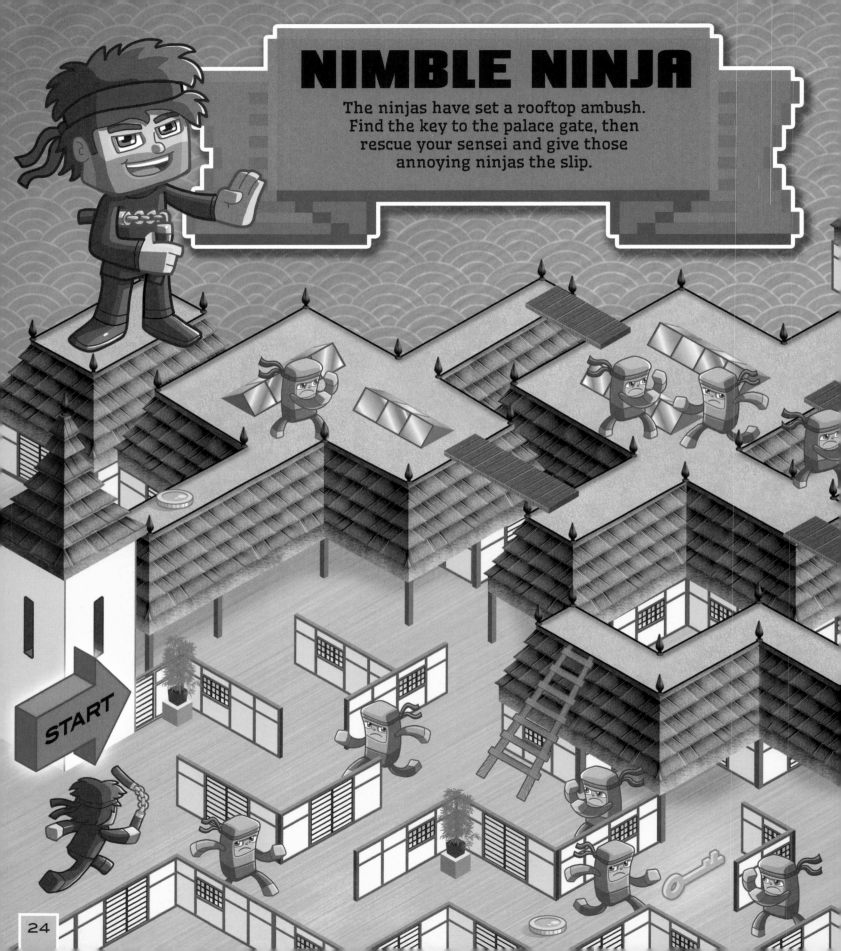

NIMBLE NINJA

The ninjas have set a rooftop ambush.
Find the key to the palace gate, then
rescue your sensei and give those
annoying ninjas the slip.

START

24

Collect all four coins along the way and check them off.

Find the key to open the gate.

FINISH

25

SPACE LAVA

Look out! This planet is full of erupting volcanoes. Gather the space flags and make your way back to the rocket.

Collect all four space flags along the way and check them off.

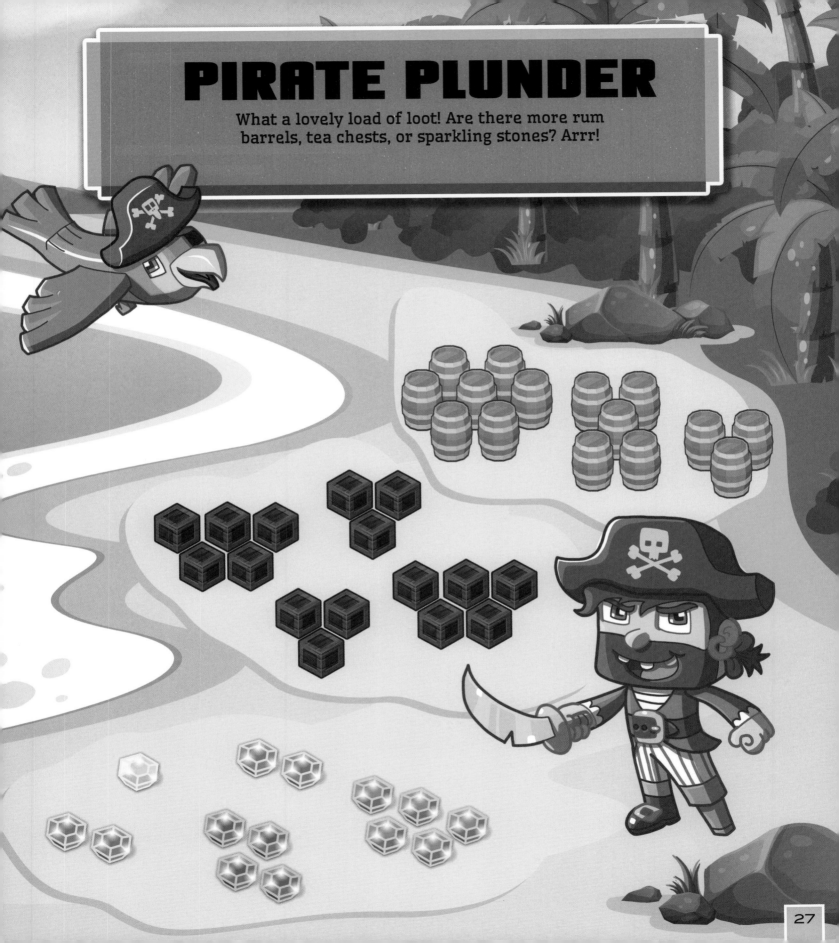

PIRATE PLUNDER

What a lovely load of loot! Are there more rum barrels, tea chests, or sparkling stones? Arrr!

Collect all four scrolls along the way and check them off.

FINISH

START

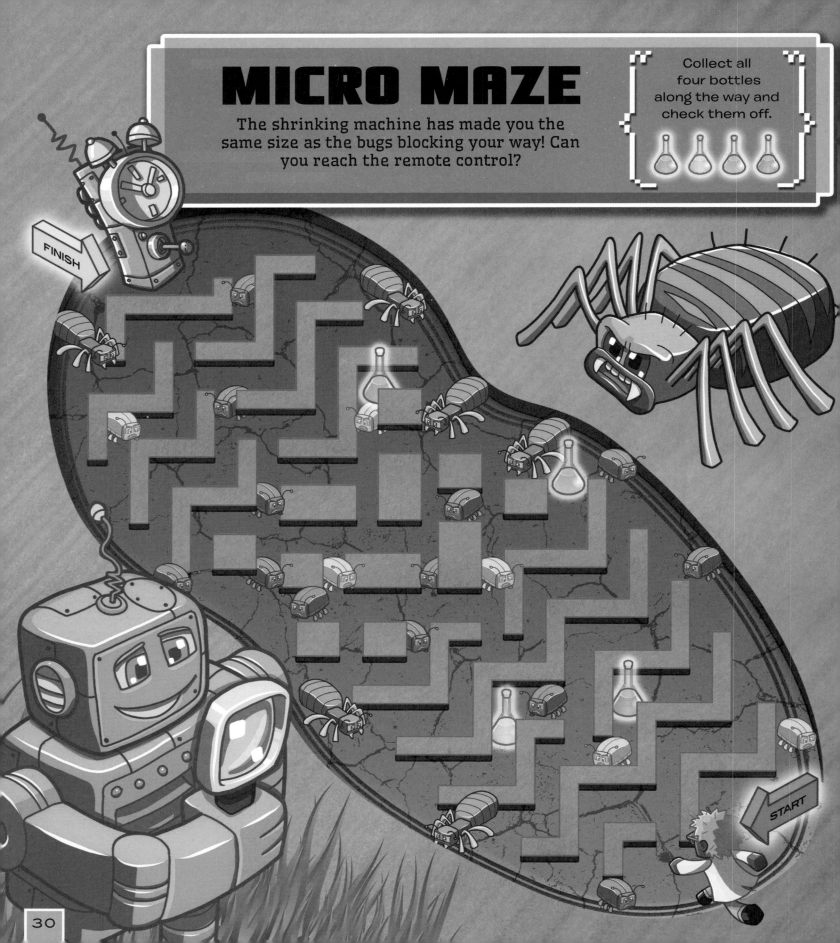

MICRO MAZE

The shrinking machine has made you the same size as the bugs blocking your way! Can you reach the remote control?

Collect all four bottles along the way and check them off.

FINISH

START

30

TANGLED UP!

Are you fishing for loot? Or just an old boot? Follow the line that's hooked to the treasure. Watch out for that shark!

SHIPWRECK!

The ship's run aground! Sneak past the pirates and giant crabs to reach the island and rescue the treasure. Find the bucket of fish to fend off the sharks.

START

RIDING RAPIDS

Ride the canoe through the rapids avoiding sharp rocks. Hang on tight, there are piranhas in there!

Collect all four gold coins along the way and check them off.

START

FINISH

SHAPE ESCAPE

Help Doc Paradox reach his robot friend. Stepping only on the six-sided stones, find a safe path across the slime-filled lab.

ASTEROIDS

Spooky space aliens have appeared from nowhere! Make your way across the asteroids to the rocket. You'll need to find a pick to clear a rockfall.

FINISH

Find a pick to break the rocks.

Collect all four space flags along the way and check them off.

START

DRAGONS' LAIR

Anna's naughty kitty, Kazam, is trapped in a lair of dragons. Find a safe path to rescue her. Beware the Dragon King!

Collect all four scrolls along the way and check them off.

START

FINISH

38

ACE FAKE

These fakes are posing as Ace McDanger,
but there's no mistaking the true original.
Connect the pairs to find the real Ace.

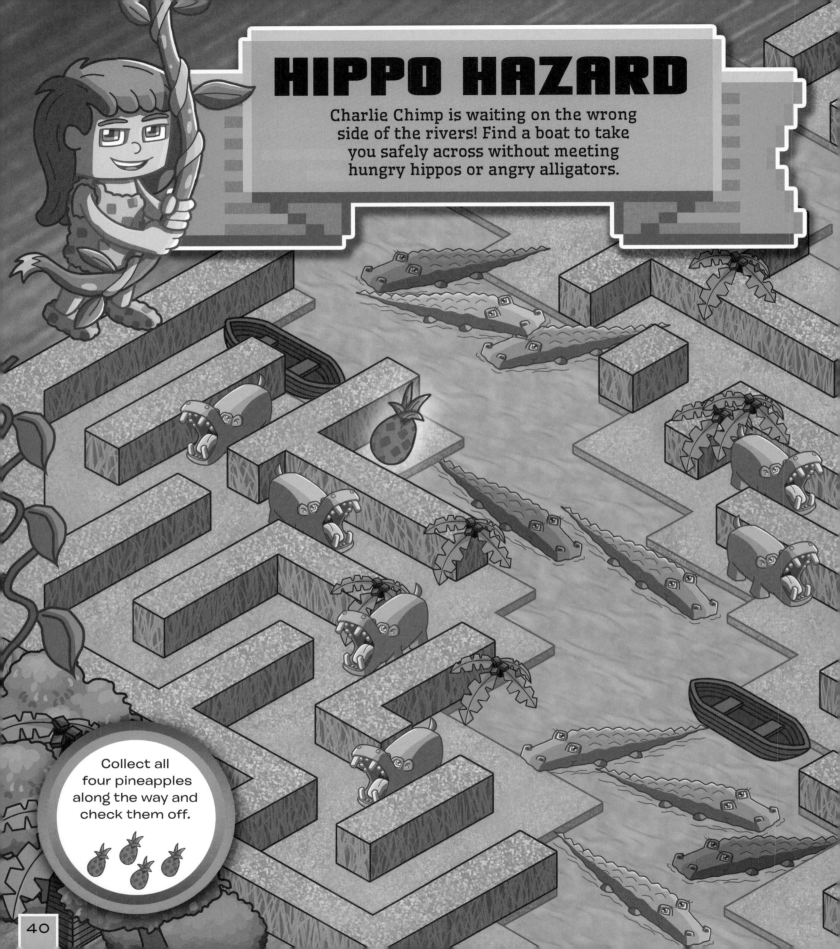

HIPPO HAZARD

Charlie Chimp is waiting on the wrong side of the rivers! Find a boat to take you safely across without meeting hungry hippos or angry alligators.

Collect all four pineapples along the way and check them off.

MAROONED!

Stuck on a desert island filled with nipping giant crabs, there's only one thing to do—find the treasure, fast!

Collect all four treasure maps along the way and check them off.

FINISH

START

42

SPELL TEST

At magic school, the students have a spell test. How will you do? Find and circle the twelve words that make six spells.

```
S H A Z A M S H
A O I W P O E U
L C Z I O P S B
A U Z Z C E A B
A S Y Z U N M L
B I M Y S I M E
R B U B B L E E
A C A D A B R A
```

1. SIM
2. SALA
3. BIM
4. HOCUS
5. POCUS
6. ABRA
7. CADABRA
8. HUBBLE
9. BUBBLE
10. SHAZAM
11. IZZY
12. WIZZY

COPY THE LEFTOVER LETTERS TO MAKE ANOTHER SPELL.

_ _ _ _ _ _ _ _ _ _ _ _

SPIDERWEB

What a sticky situation! Find a route through the giant jungle spiderweb to rescue Charlie Chimp.

Collect all four pineapples along the way and check them off.

FINISH

START

SPACE SPECKS

These molecules are about to materialize.
Connect the dots to find out who it is.

SCRAMBLE

The race is on! Steer around the course to the finish line avoiding the oil slicks and cones. Use the ramps to jump over hazards.

FINISH

Watch out for oil slicks!

48

Collect all four gold coins along the way and check them off.

START

49

SPACE BASE

Aliens have taken over the base.
Sneak back to the control room—
but don't let them spot you!

Collect all
four space flags
along the way and
check them off.

FINISH

START

SELFIE

Charlie Chimp wants a selfie with Jungle Jen. Use the grid as a guide and copy the drawing so they can both have a picture.

MAGIC LIBRARY

The trolls have invaded the library! Collect the magic scrolls, then cast a spell to escape through the door in the tower. But first, you'll need a wand.

START

JET PACK RACE

Swerve around the flying robots
as you jet through the clouds
and collect the bottles.

Collect all four bottles along the way and check them off.

FINISH

START

54

PHARAOH'S TOMB

King Kopet's tomb has been sealed for three thousand years. Why has no one tried to enter it? The symbols above the entrance may hold a clue.

CIPHER

A		K		U	
B		L		V	
C		M		W	
D		N		X	
E		O		Y	
F		P		Z	
G		Q			
H		R			
I		S			
J		T			

USE THE CIPHER ABOVE
TO CRACK THE CODE.

_ _ _ _ _ _   _ _

_ _ _ _ _ _ _ _ _ _ _

SEA MONSTER!

The treasure is locked in the captain's cabin. You'll need a boat to fetch the key on the island. Look out for the sea monsters, sharks, and giant crabs.

FINISH

EARTHQUAKE!

The Earth is shaking and volcanoes are erupting all around! Find a safe path through the maze of cracks.

Collect all four gold coins along the way and check them off.

FINISH

START

TREASURE MAP

There are false trails, traps, and dangers on Treasure Island. Use the grid to follow the map directions and reach the buried treasure chest.

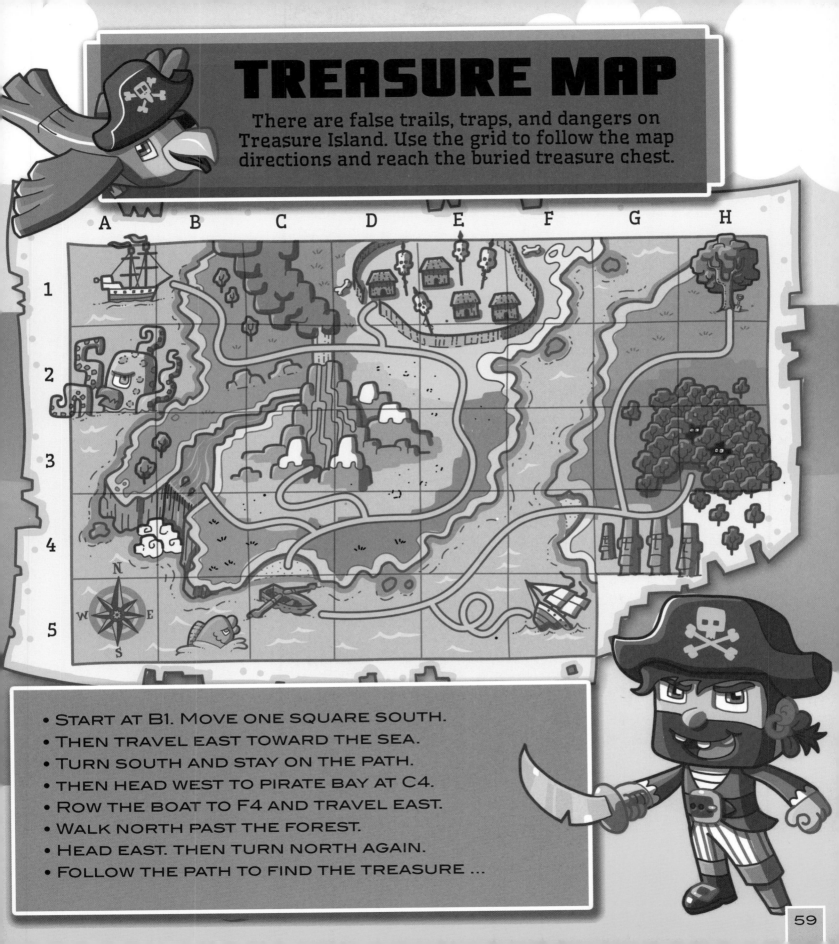

- START AT B1. MOVE ONE SQUARE SOUTH.
- THEN TRAVEL EAST TOWARD THE SEA.
- TURN SOUTH AND STAY ON THE PATH.
- THEN HEAD WEST TO PIRATE BAY AT C4.
- ROW THE BOAT TO F4 AND TRAVEL EAST.
- WALK NORTH PAST THE FOREST.
- HEAD EAST. THEN TURN NORTH AGAIN.
- FOLLOW THE PATH TO FIND THE TREASURE ...

GRAVEYARD

The skeletons are rattling their bones tonight! Gallop around the graveyard until you get to the gate, and reach safety.

Collect all four magic scrolls along the way and check them off.

START

FINISH

62

QUICK CALCULATION

Someone has left a hidden message on the white board. Work out and complete the sequences, then turn the page upside down to view the answer.

5	2	17	1	14
↓	↓	↓	↓	↓
4	5	15	3	12
↓	↓	↓	↓	↓
3	3	13	2	10
↓	↓	↓	↓	↓
2	6	11	3	8
↓	↓	↓	↓	↓
1	4	9	3	6
↓	↓	↓	↓	↓
__	__	__	__	__

WRITE THE MESSAGE HERE

__ __ __ __ __

ALIEN PLANET

It's time to leave—the aliens are coming!
Find a pick to break the space rocks
blocking the path back to the space rocket.

START

TREASURE!

Find the treasure hidden deep in the underground tunnels. Look out for pesky pirate goblins.

Collect all four treasure maps along the way and check them off.

START

FINISH

BIRTHDAY

It's someone's birthday today.
Solve the clues and find out
who is celebrating.

HAPPY BIRTHDAY to the person who ...
is standing on the floor; does not have blue eyes;
is not wearing a hat but is wearing a tie;
and is not wearing glasses.

PORTALS

The robots are running wild in the lab. Travel back through the matching portals—pink to pink, orange to orange, and so on—to reach the control panel.

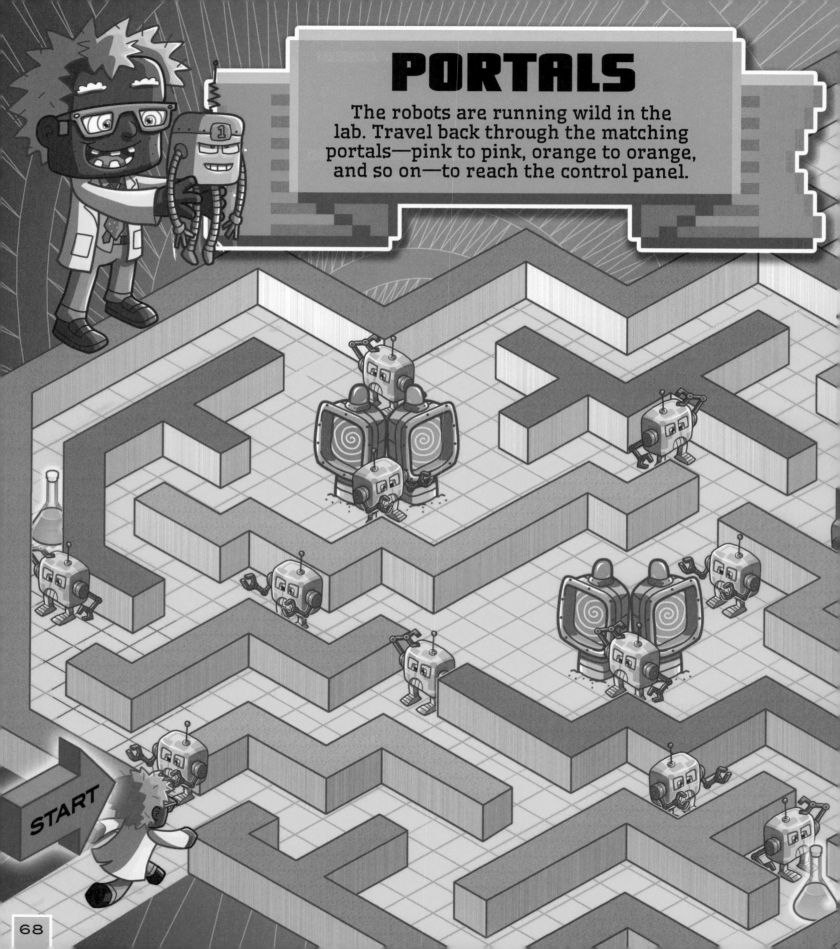

START

69

ANGRY APES!

Something's upsetting the gorillas. Get back to the treehouse without meeting an angry ape along the way.

Collect all four pineapples along the way and check them off.

START

FINISH

70

MAGIC FISH

The magic fish is swimming the wrong way.
Move just three sticks to make
the fish swim from left to right.

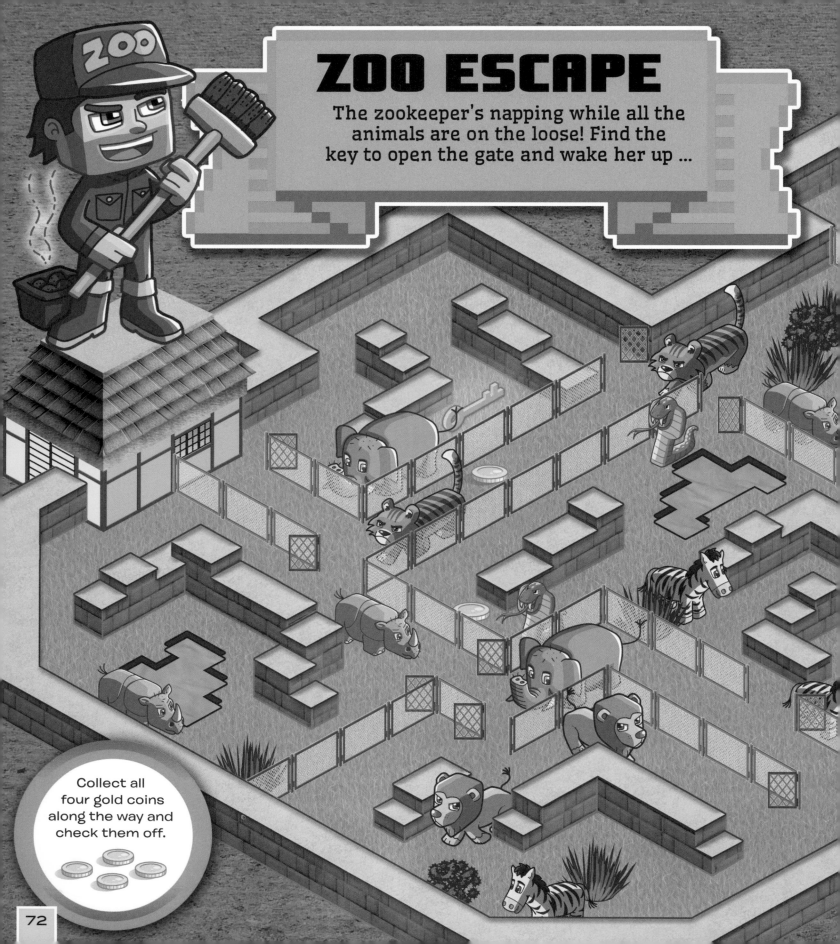

ZOO ESCAPE

The zookeeper's napping while all the animals are on the loose! Find the key to open the gate and wake her up ...

Collect all four gold coins along the way and check them off.

BLACK HOLE

A giant black hole is sucking everything toward it! Dodge the hurling comets to reach the spaceship.

Collect all four space flags along the way and check them off.

74

JUNGLE SCHOOL

Charlie Chimp is learning the alphabet.
Use crayons, pencils, or pens
to complete the picture.

Collect all four magic scrolls along the way and check them off.

START

77

CYBERSPACE

The computer's gone crazy and trapped you in a virtual maze. Find the escape portal, but don't go near those computer viruses.

Collect all four bottles along the way and check them off.

FINISH

START

SPACE RACE

The spaceship's navigation system is in a spin! Find the route to reach the planet.

PIRATE ISLE

What a bunch of brigands! Dodge the wicked pirates and hungry crocodiles to reach the ladder, retrieve the key, and unlock the treasure chest.

Collect all four treasure maps along the way and check them off.

FINISH

START

BIG BANG!

Uh-oh ... this cave is full of explosives!
Find the safe exit and make a quick escape,
but keep away from any lit fuses!

Collect all
four gold coins
along the way and
check them off.

FINISH

START

82

PARADOX PAIR

Doc Paradox has made a cloning machine,
but most of its copies are faulty!
Find the two identical clones.

TREETOP TRAIL

Fallen branches are blocking the way through the treetops. Find a saw to cut through the branches and make a path home avoiding the snakes and vultures.

FINISH

Collect all four pineapples along the way and check them off.

FULL MOON

The full moon has transformed the magic school pupils into werewolves. Rush to the cauldron for a potion to reverse the spell!

Collect all four magic scrolls along the way and check them off.

START

FINISH

PIRATE PUZZLE

There's a gold coin missing.
Find and circle twelve words to find
out who took it.

```
S H I P M A T E
P L A N K H R O
Y M P A S O E T
G P I G K Y A C
L C R O U F S H
A R A L L L U E
S E T D L A R S
S W E R R G E T
```

1. PIRATE
2. SKULL
3. GOLD
4. MAP
5. AHOY
6. PLANK
7. CREW
8. CHEST
9. FLAG
10. SHIPMATE
11. TREASURE
12. SPYGLASS

COPY THE LEFTOVER LETTERS TO
DISCOVER WHO HAS HIDDEN THE
MISSING COIN.

_ _ _ _ _ _ _

EXPEDITION SUCCESSFUL!

Ace McDanger here. I have made a guide to each part of the expedition showing safe paths to the treasure. If you followed these paths, you have completed the amazing maze adventure without difficulty!

The red path leads to the special item needed to reach your goal.

The blue path leads from the special item to the final goal.

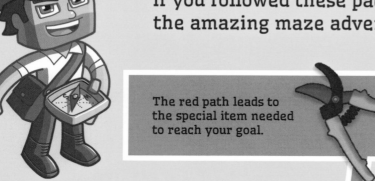

MAGIC GARDEN

The plants in this magical garden are alive ... and they look HUNGRY! Find the shears to chop down the man-eating flower blocking the exit. Beware of the prickly trees!

Collect all four magic scrolls along the way and check them off.

FINISH

START

76

77

Find the shears to cut the giant flower.

The green path shows the way to the treasure, supplies, and precious items you need to gather along the way.

Did you avoid the deadly creatures and fiendish traps?

PAGES 4/5

PAGE 6

PAGE 7

PAGES 8/9

PAGE 10

PAGE 11

PAGES 12/13

PAGE 14

PAGE 15

PAGES 16/17

PAGE 18

PAGE 19

PAGES 20/21

PAGE 22

PAGES 24/25

PAGE 26

PAGE 27

THE TEA CHESTS MAKE
THE BIGGEST BOOTY!

PAGES 28/29

PAGE 30

PAGE 31
LINE C HOOKS
THE TREASURE

PAGES 32/33

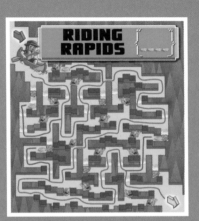

PAGE 34

PAGE 35

PAGES 36/37

PAGE 38

PAGE 39

PAGES 40/41

PAGE 42

PAGE 43

ANSWER: OPEN SESAME

PAGES 44/45

PAGE 46

PAGE 47

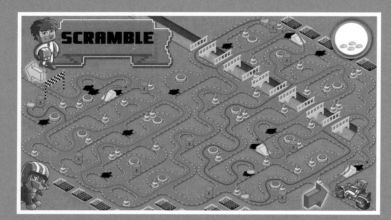

PAGES 48/49

PAGE 50

MAGIC LIBRARY

PAGES 52/53

JET PACK RACE

PAGE 54

PHARAOH'S TOMB

PAGE 55
ANSWER: A CURSE ON ALL WHO ENTER

SEA MONSTER!

PAGES 56/57

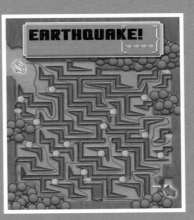

EARTHQUAKE!

PAGE 58

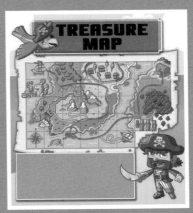

TREASURE MAP

PAGE 59
ANSWER: FIND THE TREASURE AT H1

JUNGLE JOG

PAGES 60/61

GRAVEYARD

PAGE 62

QUICK CALCULATION

PAGE 63
ANSWER: HELLO

PAGES 64/65

PAGE 66

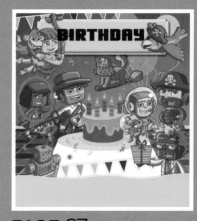

PAGE 67

ANSWER: IT'S ANNA KADABRA'S BIRTHDAY

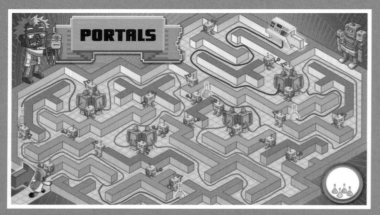

PAGES 68/69

PAGE 70

PAGE 71

PAGES 72/73

PAGE 74

PAGES 76/77

PAGE 78

PAGE 79

PAGES 80/81

PAGE 82

PAGE 83

PAGES 84/85

PAGE 86

PAGE 87
ANSWER: PARROT

JOIN OUR NEXT
EXPEDITION FOR MORE
AMAZING ADVENTURES!